JOE FLACCO, JAMAL LEWIS, SAM GASH, MICHAEL JACKSON, DERRICK MASON, TODD HEAP, JONATHAN OGDEN, ORLANDO BROWN, JEFF BLACKSHEAR, WALLY WILLIAMS, MIKE FLYNN, MICHAEL MCCRARY, ROB BURNETT, SAM ADAMS, TONY SIRAGUSA, RAY LEWIS, PETER BOULWARE, TERRELL SUGGS, CHRIS MCALISTER, DUANE STARKS, ED REED, ROD WOODSON, MATT STOVER, SAM KOCH, JOE FLACCO, JAMAL LEWIS, SAM GASH, MICHAEL JACKSON, DERRICK MASON, TODD HEAP, JONATHAN OGDEN, ORLANDO BROWN, JEFF BLACKSHEAR

THE STORY OF THE BALTIMORE RAVENS

THE STORY OF THE
BALTIMORE RAVENS

BY JIM WHITING

CREATIVE EDUCATION / CREATIVE PAPERBACKS

PUBLISHED BY CREATIVE EDUCATION AND CREATIVE PAPERBACKS
P.O. BOX 227, MANKATO, MINNESOTA 56002
CREATIVE EDUCATION AND CREATIVE PAPERBACKS ARE IMPRINTS OF THE
CREATIVE COMPANY
WWW.THECREATIVECOMPANY.US

DESIGN AND PRODUCTION BY BLUE DESIGN (WWW.BLUEDES.COM)
ART DIRECTION BY RITA MARSHALL
PRINTED IN CHINA

PHOTOGRAPHS BY AP IMAGES (ASSOCIATED PRESS), GETTY IMAGES (JUSTIN K.
ALLER, GEORGE BRIDGES/MCT, SIMON BRUTY/SI, ROB CARR, TIMOTHY A. CLARY
/AFP, JAMES DRAKE/SI, G FIUME, FOCUS ON SPORT, OTTO GREULE JR., DOUG
KAPUSTIN/MCT, ANDY LYONS/ALLSPORT, RONALD MARTINEZ, AL MESSER-
SCHMIDT, DOUG PENSINGER, TOM PIDGEON/ALLSPORT, JOE SARGENT, PATRICK
SMITH, JAMIE SQUIRE/ALLSPORT, MATT SULLIVAN, GENE SWEENEY JR./
BALTIMORE SUN/MCT, SCOTT TAETSCH, ROB TRINGALI/SPORTSCHROME, DILIP
VISHWANAT, NICK WASS)

NAMES: WHITING, JIM, AUTHOR.
TITLE: THE STORY OF THE BALTIMORE RAVENS / JIM WHITING.
SERIES: NFL TODAY.
INCLUDES INDEX.
SUMMARY: THIS HIGH-INTEREST HISTORY OF THE NATIONAL FOOTBALL
LEAGUE'S BALTIMORE RAVENS HIGHLIGHTS MEMORABLE GAMES, SUMMARIZES
SEASONAL TRIUMPHS AND DEFEATS, AND FEATURES STANDOUT PLAYERS SUCH
AS RAY LEWIS.
IDENTIFIERS: LCCN 2018059636 / ISBN 978-1-64026-132-7 (HARDCOVER) /
ISBN 978-1-62832-695-6 (PBK) / ISBN 978-1-64000-250-0 (EBOOK)
SUBJECTS: LCSH: BALTIMORE RAVENS (FOOTBALL TEAM)—HISTORY—JUVENILE
LITERATURE.
CLASSIFICATION: LCC GV956.B3 W47 2019 / DDC 796.332/64097526—DC23

FIRST EDITION HC 9 8 7 6 5 4 3 2 1
FIRST EDITION PBK 9 8 7 6 5 4 3 2 1

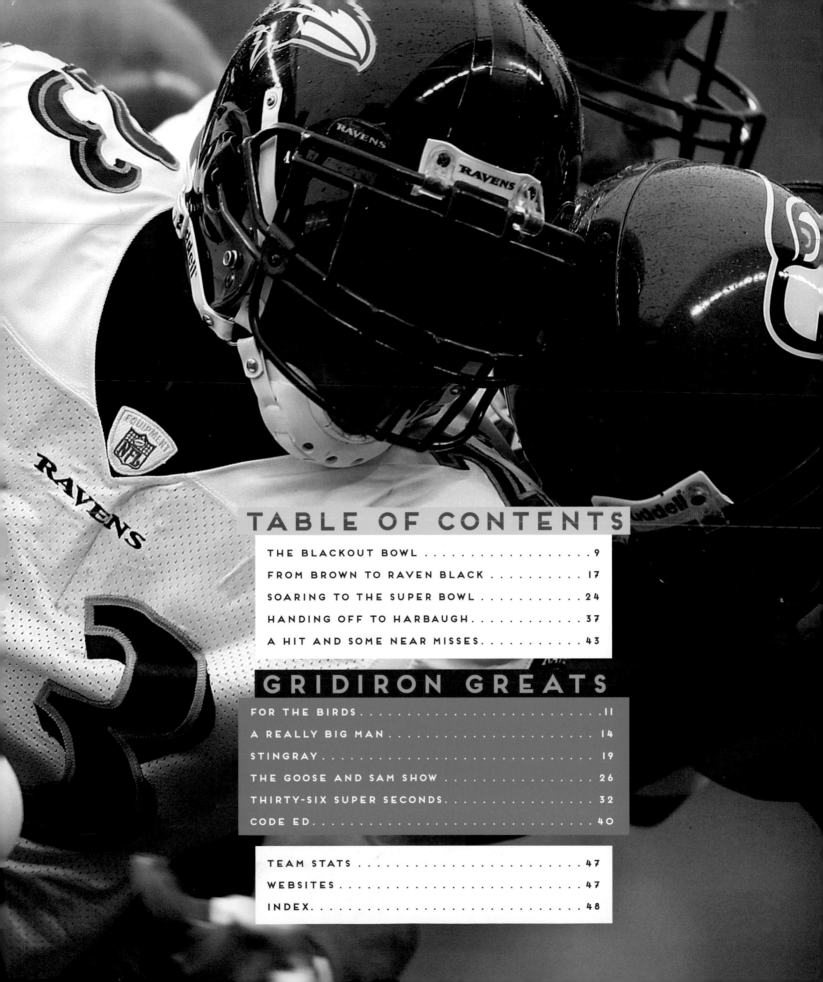

TABLE OF CONTENTS

GRIDIRON GREATS

THE BLACKOUT BOWL

Super Bowl XLVII featured the San Francisco 49ers and the Baltimore Ravens. The National Football League (NFL) Championship Game became famous for pitting brother against brother as coaches of the teams. Jim Harbaugh led the 49ers. His older brother John was the Ravens' headman. From the moment the teams were determined, the game took on many nicknames. It was dubbed the Harbowl, the Super Baugh, and the Brother Bowl. Their parents and sister became media stars. "[It was a] great feeling of joy," said their mother Jackie when the matchup was determined. "I know one is going to win and one is going to lose, but I would really like [the game] to end in a tie."

The brothers had already faced each other on Thanksgiving Day in 2011. John's Ravens won that game. But this was the Super Bowl. San Francisco was favored to win. It had a better record that year. Plus, the team had never lost a Super Bowl. It was seeking its sixth win. That would tie with the Pittsburgh Steelers for most Super Bowl victories. But the Ravens shot to an early lead. Quarterback Joe Flacco threw a 13-yard touchdown pass to wide receiver Anquan Boldin. The Niners responded with a field goal. Flacco threw two more touchdown passes in the second quarter. One went to tight end Dennis Pitta. Wide receiver Jacoby Jones caught the other. Another San Francisco field goal made the score 21–6 at halftime. Jones set a Super Bowl record early in the third quarter. He ran a kickoff 108 yards into the end zone. Baltimore's 28–6 lead made the outlook dim for San Francisco.

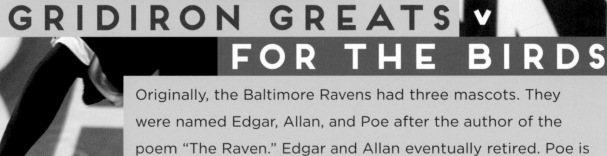

GRIDIRON GREATS v
FOR THE BIRDS

Originally, the Baltimore Ravens had three mascots. They were named Edgar, Allan, and Poe after the author of the poem "The Raven." Edgar and Allan eventually retired. Poe is the only one that remains. The team also has two real ravens. Their names are Rise and Conquer. Each bird weighs a pound and a half. Their wingspans are three and a half feet. Rise and Conquer enjoy their job. "They like to be stimulated," said Amy Eveleth. She trains the birds for their appearances. When they are done, they go back home to the Maryland Zoo.

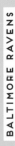

JACOBY JONES

"I KNOW ONE IS GOING TO WIN AND ONE IS GOING TO LOSE, BUT I WOULD REALLY LIKE [THE GAME] TO END IN A TIE."

—JACKIE HARBAUGH ON HER SONS MEETING IN THE SUPER BOWL

The field itself soon grew dim. An equipment failure caused many stadium lights to go out. It quickly became known as the "Blackout Bowl." Play resumed 30 minutes later. Behind quarterback Colin Kaepernick, the 49ers scored 17 points in the third quarter. Baltimore's Justin Tucker kicked a short field goal to extend the team's lead. But San Francisco narrowed the score to 31–29. It attempted a two-point conversion. But it failed.

Another Baltimore field goal gave the Ravens a 34–29 lead. Four minutes remained. San Francisco had one more chance. But it could not reach the end zone. The final score was 34–31. Baltimore had its second Super Bowl triumph!

GRIDIRON GREATS v
A REALLY BIG MAN

Even by NFL standards, Jonathan Ogden was a giant. His strength was evident, but his nimble feet made him unique. The Ravens recognized his talent. They made him the fourth overall pick in the 1996 Draft. In 2000, they rewarded him with a $44-million contract. It was the largest in league history for an offensive lineman. Opponents also thought highly of Ogden. "You have to try to keep him off-balance," said New York Giants defensive end Cedric Jones, "but he is so big and his arms are so big that it is hard to do." Ogden caught two career passes. From those passes, he compiled two total yards and two touchdowns.

11 PRO BOWL SELECTIONS

177 GAMES PLAYED

BALTIMORE COLTS QUARTERBACK
JOHNNY UNITAS

FROM BROWN TO RAVEN BLACK

T he Ravens weren't the first NFL team in Baltimore. The Baltimore Colts were founded in 1953. They brought three championship trophies to the city. In 1984, owner Robert Irsay moved the team to Indianapolis, Indiana. Art Modell owned the Cleveland Browns. In 1995, he announced that his team would move to Baltimore. It would begin playing in 1996.

Cleveland kept the Browns' name, colors, and official team records. So Baltimore needed a new identity for its "new"

99

99 CAREER TACKLES FOR LOSS

41.5

41.5 CAREER SACKS

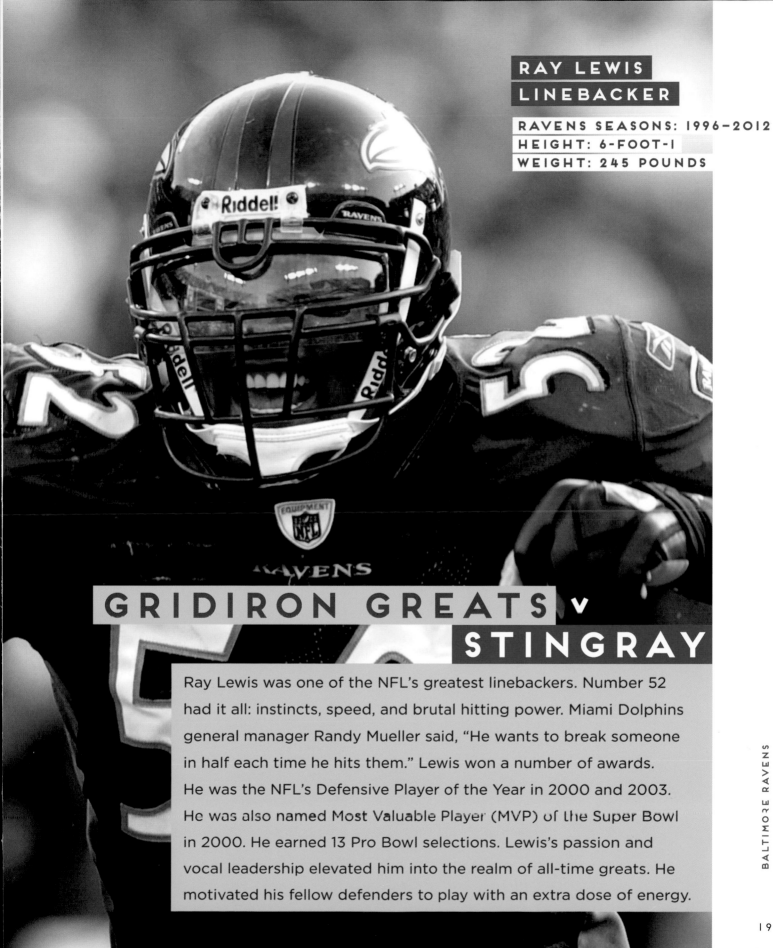

RAY LEWIS
LINEBACKER

RAVENS SEASONS: 1996–2012
HEIGHT: 6-FOOT-1
WEIGHT: 245 POUNDS

GRIDIRON GREATS v
STINGRAY

Ray Lewis was one of the NFL's greatest linebackers. Number 52 had it all: instincts, speed, and brutal hitting power. Miami Dolphins general manager Randy Mueller said, "He wants to break someone in half each time he hits them." Lewis won a number of awards. He was the NFL's Defensive Player of the Year in 2000 and 2003. He was also named Most Valuable Player (MVP) of the Super Bowl in 2000. He earned 13 Pro Bowl selections. Lewis's passion and vocal leadership elevated him into the realm of all-time greats. He motivated his fellow defenders to play with an extra dose of energy.

BALTIMORE RAVENS

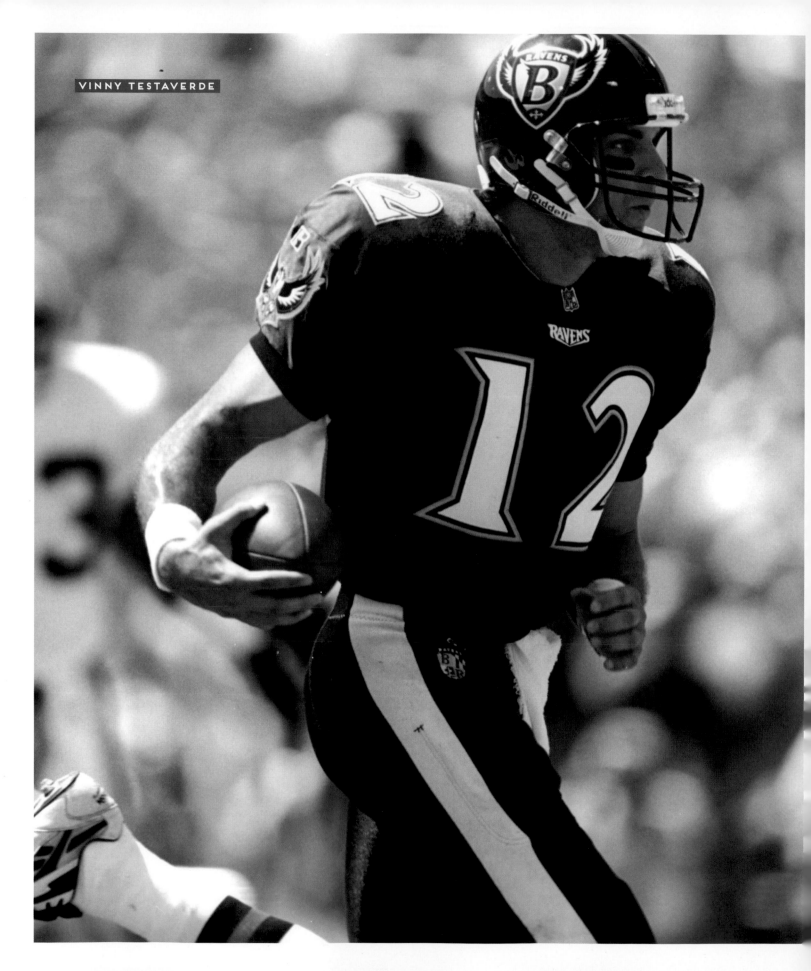
VINNY TESTAVERDE

team. A local newspaper asked residents for suggestions. Popular choices were Americans and Marauders. These names connected to the city's history. The winner, however, was taken from "The Raven." Edgar Allan Poe wrote the poem in Baltimore in 1845. In it, a raven torments a broken-hearted man. When the man starts to hope, the bird croaks, "Nevermore." This points to the man's hopeless situation.

Some people felt the incoming team was hopeless. It hadn't won an NFL championship since 1964. It had just one winning season in the past six years. But as the Ravens, the team received a boost. It had two picks in the first round of the 1996 NFL Draft. The Ravens selected tackle Jonathan Ogden. They also chose ferocious linebacker Ray Lewis. Ogden was known for his enormous strength, quick feet, and keen understanding of the game. Lewis was a tough tackler. His confidence added swagger to the defense. "They personified what playing like a Raven was about—Ray with his passion, J. O. with his attention to detail, a quiet competitor that wanted to be good every day in every way," said general manager Ozzie Newsome. "They were the foundation here."

Ogden and Lewis were key parts of that first season. Lewis made 95 tackles. Ogden allowed Vinny Testaverde to shine. The quarterback threw for 4,177 yards and 33

"THEY PERSONIFIED WHAT PLAYING LIKE A RAVEN WAS ABOUT—RAY WITH HIS PASSION, J. O. WITH HIS ATTENTION TO DETAIL."

—OZZIE NEWSOME

touchdowns. He passed for 429 yards in a game against the St. Louis Rams. Still, the team struggled. Baltimore won only four games. "We took our share of lumps this year," said coach Ted Marchibroda. "But we had a lot of young players do a lot of growing up. We'll get better."

Getting better took time. The Ravens boasted a strong defense. But they had problems scoring points. They suffered two more losing seasons. Then they hired Brian Billick as head coach in 1999. He focused on developing the team's offense. It started the season 3–6. But then the team took flight. Baltimore won five of its last seven games to finish 8–8. "We've built a little fire here," Billick said. "It will be interesting to see how big it gets."

SOARING TO THE SUPER BOWL

JAMAL LEWIS

The fire burned brightly in 2000. The Ravens had the fifth overall pick of the 2000 NFL Draft. They selected running back Jamal Lewis. He was a powerful ballcarrier. The Ravens rose to a 5–1 start. The fearsome defense led the way. It kept opponents from scoring any points in three of those six games. But the offense struggled. Baltimore went four straight games without an offensive touchdown.

Billick inserted Trent Dilfer as the starting quarterback in Week 9. The decision paid off. Dilfer led the Ravens to seven straight victories. Baltimore finished 12–4. It earned a playoff spot as a Wild Card team. Ray Lewis and

TONY "GOOSE" SIRAGUSA
DEFENSIVE TACKLE

RAVENS SEASONS: 1997–2001
HEIGHT: 6-FOOT-3
WEIGHT: 330 POUNDS

SAM ADAMS
DEFENSIVE TACKLE

RAVENS SEASONS: 2000–01
HEIGHT: 6-FOOT-3
WEIGHT: 350 POUNDS

GRIDIRON GREATS ˅
THE GOOSE AND SAM SHOW

In 2000, the Ravens' defense was one of the best in NFL history. It allowed just 10.3 points per game. It set a league record by limiting opponents to an average of 60.6 rushing yards per game. Two key players were massive defensemen Sam Adams and Tony "Goose" Siragusa. Their bulk and power enabled them to stop running backs in their tracks. Each man also drew double-team blocking. This meant Ray Lewis faced fewer blockers. Lewis once said, "We won the Super Bowl in 2000 because we had two guys in front of me that told me, 'You will not be touched.'"

2.7

2.7 YARDS ALLOWED PER RUSHING ATTEMPT (RANKED #1)

970

970 RUSHING YARDS ALLOWED (RANKED #1)

the defense had surrendered only 165 points. It was an NFL record for a 16-game season. "We're no offensive juggernaut," said tight end Shannon Sharpe. "But we don't have to be. If we score 17 points, Ray [Lewis] and the 'D' will make it stick."

The Ravens advanced to Super Bowl XXXV. Along the way, they had tackled the Denver Broncos, the Tennessee Titans, and the Oakland Raiders. They allowed just 16 total points throughout the playoffs. In the big game, Baltimore faced the New York Giants. The Giants had thrashed the Minnesota Vikings 41–0 in their last playoff game. But Baltimore scored the first points. Dilfer hit receiver Brandon Stokley with a touchdown pass in the first quarter. The Ravens' defense grabbed four interceptions. Defensive back Duane Starks returned one for a touchdown. Later, Jermaine Lewis returned a kickoff 84 yards to the end zone. Baltimore won, 34–7. The Ravens held New York to just 152 total yards. Giants'

quarterback Kerry Collins had the second-worst passer rating in Super Bowl history. Against Minnesota, he had thrown for 381 yards and 5 touchdowns. "No disrespect to Minnesota," Ray Lewis said, "but the Giants did all those good things against Minnesota. And the Giants weren't playing Minnesota's defense this week." Lewis was named the game's Most Valuable Player (MVP). It was only the second time that a linebacker had received the honor.

TRENT DILFER

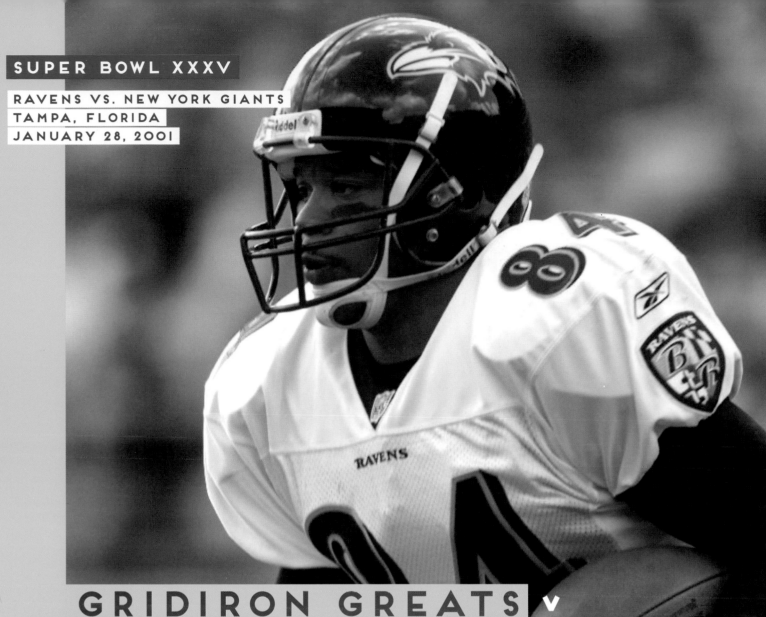

GRIDIRON GREATS v
THIRTY-SIX SUPER SECONDS

Super Bowl XXXV is noted for 36 exciting seconds. In the third quarter, Ravens cornerback Duane Starks grabbed an interception. He returned it 49 yards for a touchdown. Then the Ravens kicked off to the Giants. New York's Ron Dixon ran the length of the field for a touchdown. It was New York's only score of the game. And Baltimore immediately returned the favor. Jermaine Lewis (above) fielded the kickoff. He took it 84 yards for a touchdown. "When we ran back our kick, it fueled us," said coach Brian Billick. "And you could see the air go out of [the Giants]."

4

4 GIANTS INTERCEPTIONS THROWN

21

21 TOTAL PUNTS IN THE GAME

The Ravens suffered a serious blow the following season. Up-and-comer Jamal Lewis suffered a season-ending knee injury. It happened during training camp. However, the Ravens still won 10 games. They made the playoffs. Hopes of a Super Bowl repeat ran high. The Ravens mauled the Miami Dolphins in the Wild Card. But they lost to the Steelers the following week.

Baltimore faded to 7–9 in 2002. But in 2003, Jamal Lewis had the season of a lifetime. He rushed for an incredible 2,066 yards. It was the second-highest single season total in NFL history. The Ravens finished at 10–6. Ray Lewis won his second Defensive Player of the Year award. Safety Ed Reed and linebacker Terrell Suggs shored up the defense. But the season ended bitterly. The Titans conquered the Ravens in the playoffs.

The offense faded in 2004. Injuries added to Baltimore's troubles. The Ravens finished at 9–7. Their woes worsened in 2005. They failed to win a single game on the road. They mustered just six wins. But a turnaround was on the horizon.

JOE FLACCO

HANDING OFF TO HARBAUGH

Baltimore signed former MVP quarterback Steve McNair before the 2006 season. "I think this is a place we can win Super Bowls," he said. "That is the missing piece out of my career." His calm leadership inspired his new teammates. The Ravens started the season with a four-game winning streak. They achieved a 13–3 mark. It was their best-ever regular season record. But the offense sagged in the playoffs. Baltimore lost to Indianapolis.

The 2007 season was perhaps the most disappointing in team history. After a 4–2 start, the Ravens collapsed. They lost all but one game during the

rest of the season. The once-impenetrable defense gave up 27 points or more in eight games. Billick was fired.

Baltimore's new coach was John Harbaugh. Under his direction, the defense improved in 2008. Rookie quarterback Joe Flacco showed veteran-like poise. The Ravens began to score more points. Their 11–5 record secured a spot in the playoffs. First, they squashed the Dolphins. Then, they knocked off the Titans. They faced the Steelers in a hard-hitting American Football Conference (AFC) Championship Game. Baltimore lost, 23–14. Still, Harbaugh loved his players' effort. "I couldn't be more proud to stand with them in victory and, today, in defeat," he said.

Harbaugh stood proudly with his scrappy Ravens in 2009. Their 9–7 record earned a Wild Card berth. Baltimore beat the New England Patriots. But the following week, its only score came from Billy Cundiff's 25-yard field goal. It lost to the Colts, 20–3.

The Ravens won 12 games in 2010. It was one of the best records in the league. Anquan Boldin gave Flacco a sure-handed target down the field. Lewis, Suggs, and Reed anchored the defense. Baltimore tallied 19 interceptions. It forced 15 fumbles. The Ravens flew into the playoffs. They trounced the Kansas City Chiefs in the Wild Card. Then they met their rivals, the Steelers, in the divisional round. At halftime, the Ravens appeared to have the game under control. They held a 14-point lead. But several turnovers led to a 31–24 defeat. "We felt good at the half," said running back Ray Rice. "Our defense had them stopped, and I thought we were going to come out and handle our business. But then the situation happened— fumble, turnover, another turnover."

RAY RICE

GRIDIRON GREATS

CODE ED

Ed Reed was smaller and quieter than Ray Lewis. But he played with the same swagger and toughness. He was naturally fast and fearless. He was also intelligent. He sought a mental edge. To learn his opponents' moves, he studied game film. In 2002, Reed blocked the first two punts in Ravens history. He returned one for a touchdown. In 2004, he picked off nine passes. It was the most in the NFL that season. He returned one of them 106 yards for a touchdown. It tied for the longest scoring play in NFL history. That year, Reed was named NFL Defensive Player of the Year.

ED REED
SAFETY

RAVENS SEASONS: 2002-12
HEIGHT: 5-FOOT-11
WEIGHT: 200 POUNDS

BALTIMORE RAVENS

41

A HIT AND SOME
NEAR MISSES

The Ravens began the 2011 season by trouncing the Steelers 35–7. They played in their first-ever Thanksgiving Day game. The Harbaugh brothers, coaches for the rival teams, stood on opposite sidelines. "I think there will be one Harbaugh side that will be really happy, and there will be another Harbaugh side that will be really, really disappointed," John said before the game. "And then Mom and Dad will be torn." John's Ravens won, 16 6. They rode that momentum to the top of the AFC North Division. The Ravens returned to 12–4. Tight end Ed Dickson led a strong offense.

BALTIMORE RAVENS

ackle Haloti Ngata was dominant on defense. In the AFC Championship Game, the Ravens faced the Patriots. Baltimore fell behind. New England won, 23–20.

The Ravens won 10 games in 2012. They returned to the postseason. They brushed aside the Colts, 24–9, in the Wild Card. Then they edged the Broncos in overtime. They won the AFC championship by defeating the Patriots. That set the stage for their Super Bowl XLVII triumph.

Two years later, the Ravens were back in the playoffs. They beat the Steelers in the Wild Card round. But they lost to the Patriots the following week. That began a dry spell. Baltimore fell to 5–11 in 2015. The following year, the team went 8–8. It missed a shot at the playoffs. Toward the end of 2017, Baltimore's record sat at 9–6. To qualify for the playoffs, the Ravens needed to beat the Cincinnati Bengals in their final game. But the team was

LEFT: ANQUAN BOLDIN

HALOTI NGATA

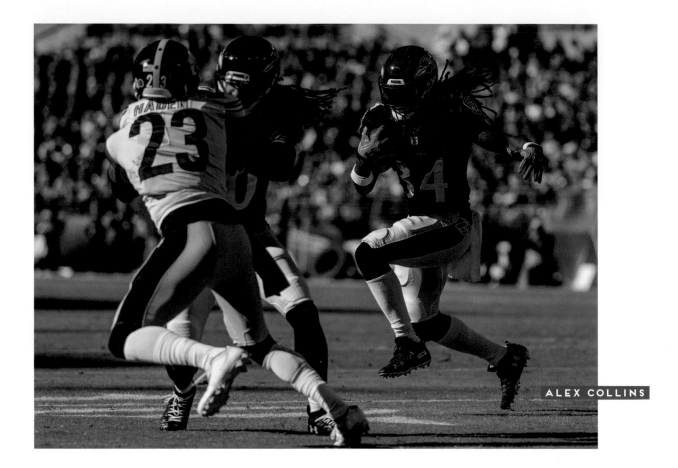

ALEX COLLINS

overcome by its own mistakes. Cincinnati won the game. Baltimore finished the season 9–7. One bright spot was Alex Collins. The running back became a cornerstone of the team. He finished with 973 rushing yards. In 2018, the Ravens flew back to the playoffs. But they fell to the Los Angeles Chargers in the Wild Card.

Exciting seasons have always been part of the Baltimore Ravens' short history. The team has established one of the most dominating defenses in NFL history. More importantly, the Ravens have brought home two Super Bowl trophies. Fans hope that the "Nevermore" croak of Edgar Allan Poe's poetic raven is wrong. When it comes to Super Bowl trophies, they want "many more."

NFL CHAMPIONSHIPS

2000, 2012

BALTIMORE RAVENS

https://www.baltimoreravens.com/

NFL: BALTIMORE RAVENS TEAM PAGE

http://www.nfl.com/teams/baltimoreravens/profile?team=BAL

BALTIMORE RAVENS

INDEX

TIGHT END TODD HEAP